The 30 Day Difference:

Make It A Habit and Make It Happen

By: Russell Stewart

Editor: Sanco Singleton Jr.

DEDICATION
THIS BOOK IS DEDICATED TO EVERYONE WHO HELPED ME CHANGE FOR THE BETTER. MAY THIS BOOK BE AN INSPIRATION TO OTHERS.

.

CONTENTS

Introduction

This book is about your life, your dreams, and your future; where you are, where you want to be, and what needs to be done to get you there. We often times become so consumed in our daily lives that we do not take the time to reflect on what it is we really want in life. We have aspirations and desires but do not have the road map that leads us there. The 30 Day Difference's objective is to challenge you to think positive, take action and build self-confidence by using a thirty day exercise. You will pick a specific goal that you want to attain and take daily steps to achieving it. I am a firm believer that if you change your habits, you will change your life. Once you've committed to being a positive thinker for thirty days, it will become second nature to be a positive, progressive, and confident individual. Let The 30 Day Difference be an inspiration to show you just how much greatness you possess.

WHAT IS A HABIT?

In order to effectively change our habits, we must begin to understand the origins of a habit. Psychologists say a habit is a thought between a stimulus and response. It is a connection mentally between a trigger thought or event, and how we respond to that trigger. Repeating this connection over time forms a habit, that affect all of the subsequent decisions . In layman's terms, habits are routine behaviors that are done on a regular basis. They are often unconscious rhythms of behavior that are continual and developed through repetition. What does this mean when it comes to achieving your goals? If there is a particular action that you are repeating but expecting a different result, then you must be insane. Insanity is defined as repeating the same action but expecting a different result or outcome. We must learn to move away from insanity and towards our destiny. Start by changing your mindset and habits. Make success a priority in your daily routine. Successful people become successful by retaining good daily habits.

How Do You Form Good Habits?

Now that you understand what a habit is, you need to know how to form good habits. Studies have shown restraining from a particular habit for thirty days is enough to break that habit. While you are not engaging in that behavior, take the time to adopt a new way to respond to that trigger or event. For example, if every morning you wake up and your first instinct is to brush your teeth, in order to break that habit you have to start waking up and washing your face. Replace your old behaviors with new behaviors in order to break and form new habits. Engaging in this change of behavior then builds momentum toward forming a new habit. When forming a new habit, it is often conscious in the beginning stages. After you have maintained thirty days of this conscious behavior it should become unconscious, thus forming a new habit.

How To Set Goals

Napoleon Hill defined goals as "Dreams with a deadline". It is the what, when and how of getting what it is you want accomplished in your life. There are 5 steps I suggest when you are setting goals. The first step is to think about the End Result and write it down on paper. The end result is asking yourself what exactly it is you want to achieve. The answers can be as general as "I want to be happy", but you must decide what your happiness looks like. You want to take time out to visualize what will your goal look like and how would you feel once you have achieved it. It is imperative that you write it down on paper, so you will have a physical attachment to what it is you are trying to accomplish. The second step is breaking your end result into small milestones. Creating milestones allow you to celebrate short-term victories as you work towards your end result. This allows you to see the proper steps you have to take to make your end result a reality. Always remember, long term goals are nothing more than achieving multiple short-term goals. The third step in creating effective goals: use the S.M.A.R.T Method to map out your strategy. You must be SPECIFIC when you are setting your goals. Answering the questions of who, what, when, where and how. Your goal has to MEASURABLE. In other words, you have to be able to keep track of your progress and calculate the steps you must take to achieve it. Next, your goal must be ATTAINABLE. Your goal should not be so farfetched that it discourages you from giving your best effort. Then you must ask yourself, are your goals RELEVANT? Your goals should add value to the bigger picture you've visualized for your life. If you do not see the worthiness in achieving your goals, chances are you won't. Lastly, you have to put a TIME frame on achieving your goals. Time frames will help you not only stay on track, but minimize your distractions. The fourth step in setting goals is having a positive attachment to whatever it is you're seeking to achieve. Positive attachments can consist of your children, affirmations, the feeling of accomplishment or whatever it may be that will keep you encouraged. You have to remain optimistic as reinforcement to getting your goals accomplished. Having a positive attachment will give you the incentive you need to be the driving force behind your efforts. The final step to setting goals is documenting and evaluating the progress of your journey. Evaluating what you are doing allows you to constantly search for better solutions to roadblocks that may occur. Now that you understand what are habits and how to set goals, you will see how they both play a part in *The 30 Day Difference*.

Russell Stewart

The 30 Day Difference: Make It A Habit And Make It Happen

The 30 Day Difference exercise consists of two very vital pieces: (1) setting a goal you would like to achieve and (2) taking daily steps to reach that goal. The objective of *The 30 Day Difference* is to get you to create good habits while working toward your goal. In the end, my hope is that you would have become more of a positive thinker and build more confidence. Pick a goal that you want to get accomplished in the next thirty days. It can be anything from a career change, to improvement of your finances or make a specific amount of sales to generate commission. Whatever you decide, your goal needs to be a measurable one. To begin, be as imaginative as you possibly can and utilize your words to paint a vivid picture of what your accomplished goal will look like. To aid you, use the guide outlined in the section "How To Set Goals". Once you've create a measurable goal you want to accomplish, EVERY MORNING for thirty days you must begin your day by reading your goal. Make it your number one priority. So before planting your feet on the floor in your bedroom, roll over, grab your workbook, and plant the seed of success in your mind. For each of your thirty days, an affirmation is provided to set a positive tone for the day. Before starting your day, you are required to fill out the objective and your four plans of action that will assist you in conquering what you desire. At the end of the day, you will journal your frustrations, resolutions, accomplishments and reflections. When you have completed your thirty days, you should have made significant progress towards or have accomplished your goal. In the midst of striving to reach your goal, you will have built the habit of thinking positive, taking action, and improving your self-confidence.

Positive Affirmations

Affirmations are positive thoughts that speak to our inner truths or beliefs. They are usually short, positive statements targeted at a specific subconscious set of beliefs used to change and undermine negative thoughts. Using positive affirmation statements empower you to stay focused on your goals and help to minimize negative distractions. When you continuously repeat positive affirmations with conviction and passion, it forces you to block negative thoughts that can manifest in your psyche. Life or death lie in the power of the tongue, therefore it is imperative that you speak nothing but positivity into your life. Reading a positive affirmation daily will help you create the habit of thinking positive during *The 30 Day Difference.*

Objective

An objective is a proposed goal or accomplishment that one is trying to attain. Each day you are required to create an objective, that upon completion will be a stepping stone that will help you get closer to your thirty day goal. Having a daily objective will allow you to dissect your overall goal and break it down day-by-day; focusing on the smaller pieces that together make your main goal. Meeting these objectives daily will help you build momentum towards your proposed goal during *The 30 Day Difference.*

Action Plan

An action plan is the process that will help you to focus your ideas to decide what steps are needed to meet your objective. The four action plans that you create daily are how you measure achieving your objective. They have to be relevant and achievable during the course of your day. If you fall short, do not be discouraged. Give your best effort in trying to complete them and document where you stumble. Remember, although you are working to achieve a goal this is a learning lesson. Completing your daily actions plans are going to create the habit of taking action during *The 30 Day Difference*

Frustrations

Frustrations can be best described as having a feeling of unfulfilled needs or an unresolved problem. Frustration gives you a feeling of dissatisfaction that often can be accompanied by anxiety or depression. When you are attempting to achieve your goals, you may run across dilemmas or distractions that may cause you to be frustrated. During your thirty day exercise, document your frustrations as a tool to help identify the causes and in order to be more proactive in minimizing these feelings and barriers. Recording your frustrations make you aware of the challenges that you face and must overcome during *The 30 Day Difference.*

Resolutions

The act of solving a problem, dispute or continuous action is a resolution. Resolutions are key when finding the solutions to unraveling your frustrations. Though you may acknowledge your frustrations, your primary focus is to provide an answer to your hindrances. Clarifying your resolutions will give you a broad prospective and insight on possible directions to take to meet your objectives. Determining your resolution helps you create a habit of strategizing to minimize the difficulties that may come your way. Placing your attention on the resolution is going to require you to think how and not why during *The 30 Day of Difference*.

Accomplishments

An accomplishment is anything that is achieved successfully. Often times we complain about what it is we do wrong and do not recognize what we do correctly. It is vital that you acknowledge your accomplishments in order to have awareness on the things you attain. You want to give your best efforts during this thirty day exercise. As a way to keep yourself motivated, focus more on what you get accomplished. *The 30 Day Difference* is more about getting objectives accomplished. It will also center around what you can do better to ensure success in creating good habits and goal completion.

Reflections

Reflection, giving serious thought or consideration to a particular subject or idea. After you've set your daily objective, work your action plan, journal your frustrations and resolutions, and list your accomplishments, you are going to give your reflections. Your overall daily reflection will focus on how you feel and what you could have done better concerning your daily objective. Everyday you are going to look back on your activities and provide yourself with the feedback you need to express how you felt and how you can improve. Focus strictly on the positives, because your reflections are going to create a habit of building self-confidence during *The 30 Day Difference*.

Russell Stewart

Time to Make A Difference in Your Life!

Now it is time for you to start *The 30 Day Difference!* Many challenges may occur during this thirty day process, but make sure that you stick it through and give 100% effort. It is important that you do not miss a day and stay consistent for thirty days to create new patterns of behavior. If for some reason you skip a day, you must start over from the beginning in order for this to be effective. The objective of this exercise is to be consistent in working toward your goal so you can develop habits to apply in all aspects of your life. Stay the course, be encouraged, and give yourself positive critiques. For the next thirty days you are going to try and eliminate negativity in your life by staying dedicated. You have to form a sense of tunnel vision to minimize all of your distractions. If you do not finish this challenge, your goal was either not worthy enough or you tried to negotiate the effort it took to complete the exercise. Good luck to you, and I wish you the best as you strive to make a difference in the next thirty days. LETS BEGIN!!!

The 30 Day Difference Goal

_____

_____

_____

_____

_____

_____

_____

_____

_____

_____

_____

_____

_____

_____

_____

_____

_____

_____

_____

_____

_____

_____

_____

_____

_____

_____

_____

_____

_____

_____

_____

_____

_____

_____

_____

_____

_____

_____

_____

_____

_____

_____

_____

_____

_____

_____

_____

_____

_____

_____

_____

_____

Day 1
"My grateful heart is a magnet that attracts all that I may desire"

Objective: _____
_____
_____

Plan Of Action:
1)

2)

3)

4)

Frustrations: _____
_____
_____

Resolutions: _____
_____
_____

Accomplishments: _____
_____
_____

Reflections: _____
_____
_____
_____

Day 2

"Once you replace negative thoughts with positive ones, you'll start having positive results." – Willie Nelson

Objective: _____

_____

_____

Plan Of Action:

1)

2)

3)

4)

Frustrations: _____

_____

_____

_____

Resolutions: _____

_____

_____

_____

Accomplishments: _____

_____

_____

_____

Reflections: _____

_____

_____

_____

Day 3

"Positive thinking will let you do everything better than negative thinking will" – Zig Ziglar

Objective: _____
_____

Plan Of Action:

1)

2)

3)

4)

Frustrations: _____
_____
_____

Resolutions: _____
_____
_____

Accomplishments: _____
_____
_____

Reflections: _____
_____
_____

Day 4
"Winners make a habit of manufacturing their own positive expectations in advance of the event"— Brain Tracy

Objective: _____

_____

_____

Plan Of Action:
1)

2)

3)

4)

Frustrations: _____

_____

_____

_____

Resolutions: _____

_____

_____

_____

Accomplishments: _____

_____

_____

_____

Reflections: _____

_____

_____

_____

Day 5

"Happiness does not lie in happiness, but in the achievement of it."-
Fyodor Dostoevsky

Objective: _____

_____

_____

Plan Of Action:
1)

2)

3)

4)

Frustrations: _____

_____

_____

_____

Resolutions: _____

_____

_____

_____

Accomplishments: _____

_____

_____

Reflections: _____

_____

_____

_____

Day 6
"Definiteness of purpose is the starting point of all achievement."
-W. Clement Stone

Objective: _____
_____
_____

Plan Of Action:
1)

2)

3)

4)

Frustrations: _____
_____
_____
_____

Resolutions: _____
_____
_____
_____

Accomplishments: _____
_____
_____
_____

Reflections: _____
_____
_____
_____

Day 7

"A dream becomes a goal when action is taken toward its achievement." - Bo Bennett

Objective: _____

_____

_____

Plan Of Action:

1)

2)

3)

4)

Frustrations: _____

_____

_____

_____

Resolutions: _____

_____

_____

_____

Accomplishments: _____

_____

_____

_____

Reflections: _____

_____

_____

_____

Day 8
"A change in bad habits leads to a change in life."

-Jenny Craig

Objective: _____
_____
_____

Plan Of Action:
1)

2)

3)

4)

Frustrations: _____
_____
_____

Resolutions: _____
_____
_____

Accomplishments: _____
_____
_____

Reflections: _____
_____
_____

Day 9

"Obstacles are those frightful things you see when you take your eyes off your goal." -Henry Ford

Objective: _____

_____

_____

Plan Of Action:

1)

2)

3)

4)

Frustrations: _____

_____

_____

Resolutions: _____

_____

_____

Accomplishments: _____

_____

_____

Reflections: _____

_____

_____

Day 10
"Glory lies in the attempt to reach one's goal and not in reaching it."
-Mahatma Gandhi

Objective: _____

_____

_____

Plan Of Action:
1)

2)

3)

4)

Frustrations: _____

_____

_____

Resolutions: _____

_____

_____

Accomplishments: _____

_____

_____

Reflections: _____

_____

_____

Day 11

"Nothing builds self-esteem and self-confidence like accomplishment."-
Thomas Carlyle

Objective: _____

_____

Plan Of Action:
1)

2)

3)

4)

Frustrations: _____

_____

_____

Resolutions: _____

_____

_____

Accomplishments: _____

_____

_____

Reflections: _____

_____

_____

Day 12

"With realization of one's own potential and self-confidence in one's ability, one can build a better world." -Dalai Lama

Objective: _____

_____

_____

Plan Of Action:

1)

2)

3)

4)

Frustrations: _____

_____

_____

Resolutions: _____

_____

_____

Accomplishments: _____

_____

_____

Reflections: _____

_____

_____

Day 13

"Don't let others put thoughts into your mind that takes away your self-confidence."- Katori Hall

Objective:
_____
_____

Plan Of Action:
1)

2)

3)

4)

Frustrations:
_____
_____
_____

Resolutions:
_____
_____
_____

Accomplishments:
_____
_____
_____

Reflections:
_____
_____
_____

Day 14

"In order to succeed, your desire for success should be greater than your fear of failure." -Bill Cosby

Objective: _____

_____

_____

Plan Of Action:
1)

2)

3)

4)

Frustrations: _____

_____

_____

Resolutions: _____

_____

_____

Accomplishments: _____

_____

_____

Reflections: _____

_____

_____

Day 15

"Try not to become a man of success, but rather try to become a man of value." -Albert Einstein

Objective: _____

_____

_____

Plan Of Action:

1)

2)

3)

4)

Frustrations: _____

_____

_____

_____

Resolutions: _____

_____

_____

_____

Accomplishments: _____

_____

_____

_____

Reflections: _____

_____

_____

_____

Day 16

"Don't aim for success if you want it; just do what you love and believe in, and it will come naturally." -David Frost

Objective: _____

_____

_____

Plan Of Action:

1)

2)

3)

4)

Frustrations: _____

_____

_____

_____

Resolutions: _____

_____

_____

_____

Accomplishments: _____

_____

_____

_____

Reflections: _____

_____

_____

_____

Day 17

"Formal education will make you a living; self-education will make you a fortune." - Jim Rohn

Objective: _____

_____

Plan Of Action:

1)

2)

3)

4)

Frustrations: _____

_____

_____

Resolutions: _____

_____

_____

Accomplishments: _____

_____

_____

Reflections: _____

_____

_____

Day 18
"Action is the foundational key to all success." - Pablo Picasso

Objective: _____

_____

Plan Of Action:
1)

2)

3)

4)

Frustrations: _____

_____

_____

Resolutions: _____

_____

_____

Accomplishments: _____

_____

_____

Reflections: _____

_____

_____

Day 19

"Failure is success if we learn from it." - Malcolm Forbes

Objective: _____

_____

_____

Plan Of Action:
1)

2)

3)

4)

Frustrations: _____

_____

_____

_____

Resolutions: _____

_____

_____

_____

Accomplishments: _____

_____

_____

_____

Reflections: _____

_____

_____

_____

Day 20

"Frustration, although quite painful at times, is a very positive and essential part of success." -Bo Bennett

Objective: _____

_____

Plan Of Action:
1)

2)

3)

4)

Frustrations: _____

_____

_____

Resolutions: _____

_____

_____

Accomplishments: _____

_____

_____

Reflections: _____

_____

_____

Day 21

"Success is getting what you want. Happiness is wanting what you get."- Dale Carnegie

Objective: _____
_____
_____

Plan Of Action:
1)

2)

3)

4)

Frustrations: _____
_____
_____
_____

Resolutions: _____
_____
_____

Accomplishments: _____
_____
_____

Reflections: _____
_____
_____
_____

Day 22
"Winning isn't everything, it's the only thing." -Vince Lombardi

Objective: _____

_____

Plan Of Action:
1)

2)

3)

4)

Frustrations: _____

_____

_____

Resolutions: _____

_____

_____

Accomplishments: _____

_____

_____

Reflections: _____

_____

_____

Day 23

"Success comes from knowing that you did your best to become the best that you are capable of becoming." -John Wooden

Objective: _____

_____

_____

Plan Of Action:

1)

2)

3)

4)

Frustrations: _____

_____

_____

_____

Resolutions: _____

_____

_____

_____

Accomplishments: _____

_____

_____

_____

Reflections: _____

_____

_____

_____

Day 24

"Destiny is not a matter of chance; but a matter of choice. It is not a thing to be waited for, It is a thing to be achieved."–William J Bryan

Objective: _____

_____

_____

Plan Of Action:

1)

2)

3)

4)

Frustrations: _____

_____

_____

Resolutions: _____

_____

_____

Accomplishments: _____

_____

_____

Reflections: _____

_____

_____

_____

Day 25

"Patience, persistence and perspiration make an unbeatable combination for success." -Napoleon Hill

Objective: _____

_____

_____

Plan Of Action:

1)

2)

3)

4)

Frustrations: _____

_____

_____

_____

Resolutions: _____

_____

_____

_____

Accomplishments: _____

_____

_____

_____

Reflections: _____

_____

_____

_____

Day 26
"Remind yourself. Nobody built like you, you design yourself."
-Jay Z

Objective: _____

_____

_____

Plan Of Action:
1)

2)

3)

4)

Frustrations: _____

_____

_____

_____

Resolutions: _____

_____

_____

_____

Accomplishments: _____

_____

_____

_____

Reflections: _____

_____

_____

_____

Day 27

"Faith is taking the first step even when you don't see the whole staircase." Martin Luther King, Jr.

Objective: _____
_____
_____

Plan Of Action:
1)

2)

3)

4)

Frustrations: _____
_____
_____

Resolutions: _____
_____
_____

Accomplishments: _____
_____
_____

Reflections: _____
_____
_____

Day 28

"Optimism is the faith that leads to achievement. Nothing can be done without hope and confidence."-Helen Keller

Objective: _____

_____

_____

Plan Of Action:

1)

2)

3)

4)

Frustrations: _____

_____

_____

_____

Resolutions: _____

_____

_____

_____

Accomplishments: _____

_____

_____

_____

Reflections: _____

_____

_____

_____

Day 29
"Successful people are simply those with successful habits."
-Brian Tracy

Objective: _____

_____

Plan Of Action:
1)

2)

3)

4)

Frustrations: _____

_____

_____

Resolutions: _____

_____

_____

Accomplishments: _____

_____

_____

Reflections: _____

_____

_____

Day 30
"We first make our habits, and then our habits make us."
-John Dryden

Objective: _____
_____
_____

Plan Of Action:
1)

2)

3)

4)

Frustrations: _____
_____
_____

Resolutions: _____
_____
_____

Accomplishments: _____
_____
_____

Reflections: _____
_____
_____

CONGRATULATIONS

Congratulations on completing *The 30 Day Difference*. I am sure that if you followed the instructions correctly you have developed the habits of positive thinking, taking action, and building self-confidence. In "The Strangest Secret", Earl Nightingale defines success as the progressive realization of a worthy ideal. This means anyone that is working toward a predetermined goal is considered successful. Now that you know how to visualize, form habits, set goals and apply strategies, imagine what other areas these tools can be applied in your life. If you did not achieve your goal, I am sure you are closer than you have ever been to attaining it. Now that you have created a habit, you should have no problems continuing to work towards accomplishing it. When you control your thoughts, you then control your life. I hope this book was a blessing to you and a difference was made in your thirty day experience. I would love to hear your testimony and your experiences from this process. Feel free to email me at info@russellqstewart.com. I wish you all the success and always remember, change your habit and change your life!

ABOUT THE AUTHOR

Raised in Lugoff, South Carolina, Russell Stewart aspired to have a life of success just like many of us eventually, achieving "The American Dream". At an early age, Russell understood the impact that poor decisions and habits could have on one's life. January 1st of each year, Russell makes a 30 day commitment to get a head start on achieving his yearly goals. In these 30 days, he eliminates all of his distractions, develops a plan and shifts his focus toward pursuing a worthy cause.

Stewart conducts financial workshops trainings along the east coast in hopes of educating individuals on the principles they need to become financially independent. Stewart's audiences have included The Talented Tenth Young Professionals Conference, The Annual African American Student Leadership Conference, SC Department of Transportation, The Cooperative Ministry, and a host of religious organizations. Over the years, Stewart has appeared on WLTX News 19's "Money Savings Monday" Fox 57's "Good Day Columbia", Charlotte's Access Channel 21's "Before the Hype", "The Minority Eye's "Most Interesting Minorities of 2014" and The SC Black Pages 40 Under 40 class of 2015".

Russell currently is the Principal and Owner of The Merrick Financial Group, LLC in Charlotte, North Carolina. Stewart is committed to the idea of helping his clients improve their financial situation. He is a creative and strategic financial service professional who has helped individuals and business owners identify and reach their unique financial objectives. Russell and his support network provide a wide-ranging services including estate planning, retirement strategies, insurance and investment reviews and specialized services for business owners.

Russell a 2008 graduate of Claflin University in Orangeburg, South Carolina, where he graduated Cum Laude with a Bachelors of Science in Human Performance and Recreation.

www.ingramcontent.com/pod-product-compliance
Lightning Source LLC
Chambersburg PA
CBHW072039060426
42449CB00010BA/2352